D1226328

THE FIVE SENSES

Touching

by Lisa Owings

BLASTOFF! READERS 3

BELLWETHER MEDIA • MINNEAPOLIS, MN

Note to Librarians, Teachers, and Parents:

**Blastoff! Readers** are carefully developed by literacy experts and combine standards-based content with developmentally appropriate text.

**Level 1** provides the most support through repetition of high-frequency words, light text, predictable sentence patterns, and strong visual support.

**Level 2** offers early readers a bit more challenge through varied simple sentences, increased text load, and less repetition of high-frequency words.

**Level 3** advances early-fluent readers toward fluency through increased text and concept load, less reliance on visuals, longer sentences, and more literary language.

**Level 4** builds reading stamina by providing more text per page, increased use of punctuation, greater variation in sentence patterns, and increasingly challenging vocabulary.

**Level 5** encourages children to move from "learning to read" to "reading to learn" by providing even more text, varied writing styles, and less familiar topics.

Whichever book is right for your reader, Blastoff! Readers are the perfect books to build confidence and encourage a love of reading that will last a lifetime!

This edition first published in 2018 by Bellwether Media, Inc.

No part of this publication may be reproduced in whole or in part without written permission of the publisher. For information regarding permission, write to Bellwether Media, Inc., Attention: Permissions Department, 5357 Penn Avenue South, Minneapolis, MN 55419.

Library of Congress Cataloging-in-Publication Data

Names: Owings, Lisa, author.
Title: Touching / by Lisa Owings.
Description: Minneapolis, MN : Bellwether Media, Inc., [2018] | Series: Blastoff! Readers. The Five Senses |
    Audience: Age 5-8. | Audience: K to Grade 3. | Includes bibliographical references and index.
Identifiers: LCCN 2017029561 | ISBN 9781626177727 (hardcover : alk. paper) ) |
    ISBN 9781618913005 (paperback : alk. paper) | ISBN 9781681034812 (ebook)
Subjects: LCSH: Touch–Juvenile literature. | Senses and sensation–Juvenile literature.
Classification: LCC QP451 .O95 2018 | DDC 612.8–dc23
LC record available at https://lccn.loc.gov/2017029561

Text copyright © 2018 by Bellwether Media, Inc. BLASTOFF! READERS and associated logos are trademarks and/or registered trademarks of Bellwether Media, Inc. SCHOLASTIC, CHILDREN'S PRESS, and associated logos are trademarks and/or registered trademarks of Scholastic Inc., 557 Broadway, New York, NY 10012.

Editor: Rebecca Sabelko     Designer: Lois Stanfield

Printed in the United States of America, North Mankato, MN.

# Table of Contents

It is low tide! This is your favorite time to walk the beach. Your feet sink into soft sand. Cool waves splash your legs.

Every few feet, you pick up a shell or stone.

5

The stones are flat and smooth. Most shells are sharp and broken. A few are still perfect.

You slip them into your bag. The sun feels warm on your shoulders as you head home.

# What Is Touching?

Skin is the largest **organ** in our bodies. Its millions of touch **receptors** connect us with the world.

Different types of receptors
let us understand touch in
many ways.

**Mechanoreceptors** in the top layers of skin sense **pressure**. Deeper down, these cells feel **vibration**.

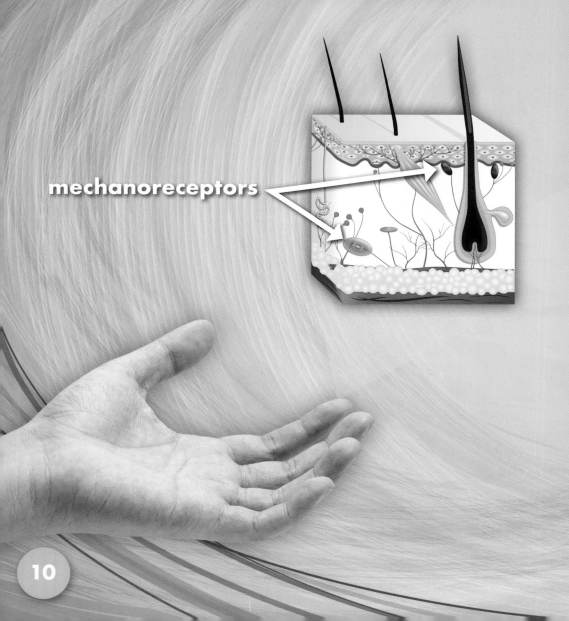

mechanoreceptors

Fingertips have the most mechanoreceptors. With them, we can feel the finest **textures** and smallest shapes. It is like seeing with our hands!

**Thermoreceptors** also live in the top layers of skin. These cells tell us the **temperature** of anything our skin touches.

When we are wounded, it hurts!
**Nociceptors** throughout the
body sense pain.

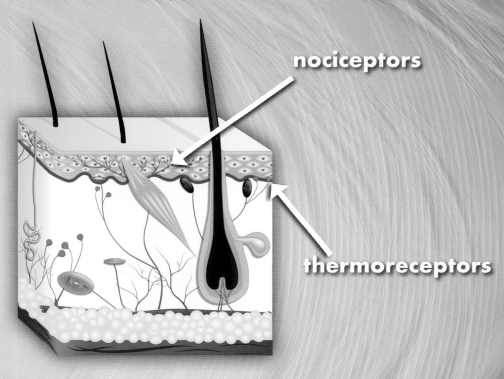

nociceptors

thermoreceptors

Touch receptors send their messages along **nerves**. These messages travel up the **spine** to the brain.

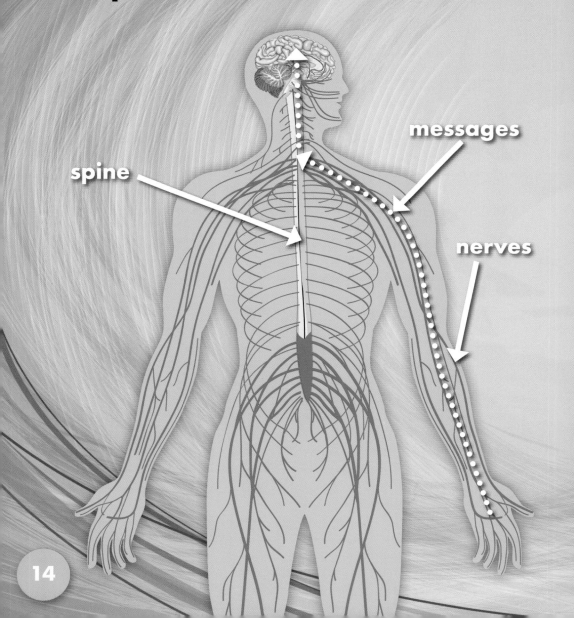

messages

spine

nerves

The messages let us feel textures
and movements down to the
tiniest tickle.

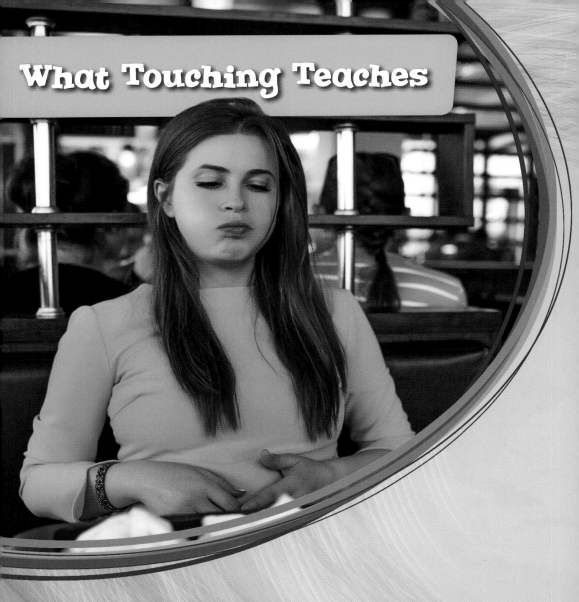

Touching offers many different lessons. Pain is a memorable feeling. The brain warns us against repeating painful experiences.

When we feel pain, **reflexes** jerk our bodies away. Pain is no fun, but it protects us.

Our bodies also need to stay the right temperature. Touch tells us if we need to wear a jacket or get out of the sun.

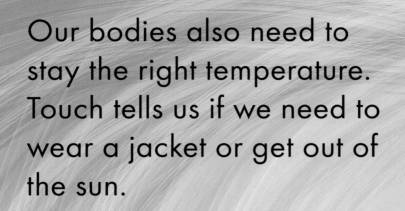

We move our bodies by feel, too. Touch receptors help us control our movements and sense where we are.

Touch affects more than just our bodies. We also need it to keep our minds healthy and happy. We are always in touch with our surroundings. Get comfortable in your skin and feel the world around you!

# Reading by Touch

**People who are blind read by touch. Can you?**

Let a friend think of a word or picture. Have them use a finger to draw it on different parts of your body. Your palm or arm are good places. Now guess what they drew.

- What did you notice?

**Extra credit**

Head to the library. Check out some books about braille. Can you learn the braille alphabet?

# Glossary

**mechanoreceptors**—receptors that sense pressure and vibration

**nerves**—threadlike structures that pass messages between the brain and the rest of the body

**nociceptors**—receptors that sense pain

**organ**—a part of the body that has a certain purpose; the skin, heart, and lungs are organs.

**pressure**—the feeling created by pressing on something

**receptors**—special cells that react to touch or other things in the outside world; receptors send messages about the outside world to the brain.

**reflexes**—movements that happen without thought or control, such as jerking your hand away from something hot; reflexes help keep us safe.

**spine**—a line of bones around a group of nerves that runs along the back

**temperature**—how hot or cold something is

**textures**—the ways surfaces can feel, such as hard, soft, bumpy, or smooth

**thermoreceptors**—receptors that sense temperature

**vibration**—movement caused by something moving quickly back and forth

# To Learn More

**AT THE LIBRARY**

Fretland VanVoorst, Jenny. *Skin*. New York, N.Y.: AV2 by Weigl, 2017.

Ganeri, Anita. *Touch*. Mankato, Minn.: A+/Smart Apple Media, 2013.

Lay, Kathryn. *Touching Their Prey: Animals with an Amazing Sense of Touch*. Minneapolis, Minn.: Magic Wagon, 2013.

**ON THE WEB**

Learning more about touching is as easy as 1, 2, 3.

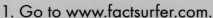

1. Go to www.factsurfer.com.

2. Enter "touching" into the search box.

3. Click the "Surf" button and you will see a list of related web sites.

With factsurfer.com, finding more information is just a click away.

# Index

The images in this book are reproduced through the courtesy of: melis, Cover; ARIMAG, pp. 4-5, 7; M. Hencher, p. 5; Davdeka, p. 6; A3pfamily, pp. 8-9; ViChizh, p. 9; Designua, pp. 10, 13; chuanpis, p. 11; FabrikaSimf, p. 12; Nygraphic, pp. 10 (hand), 13 (hand); Vecton, p. 14; marina_eno1, p. 15; stock_colors, p. 16; Phovoir, p. 17; unguryanu, p. 18 (top); Tachjang, p. 18 (bottom); Izf, pp. 18-19; Beneda Miroslav, p. 20; Maica, p. 21.